DESTINATION Middle Ages

Your Guide to Castles and Medieval Warfare

James Bow

Crabtree Publishing Company
www.crabtreebooks.com

Crabtree Publishing Company
www.crabtreebooks.com

Author: James Bow

Managing Editor: Tim Cooke

Designer: Lynne Lennon

Picture Manager: Sophie Mortimer

Design Manager: Keith Davis

Editorial Director: Lindsey Lowe

Children's Publisher: Anne O'Daly

Editor: Petrice Custance

Proofreader: Wendy Scavuzzo

**Production coordinator
   and prepress technician:** Tammy McGarr

Print coordinator: Margaret Amy Salter

Written and produced for Crabtree Publishing Company
by Brown Bear Books

Photographs (t=top, b=bottom, l=left, r=right, c=center):
Front Cover: Public Domain: main, cr; **Shutterstock:** tr;
Thinkstock: istockphoto br.

Interior: Alamy: Falkensteinfoto 15b, Florilegius 4bl, Interfoto 20;
Musée de l'Armée: Gallimard 11c; **Billeder af Norges Historie
tegnede:** 9t; Bridgeman Art Library: 29tr, Bibliotheque Nationale
123bl;
Bruges Garter Book: William Bruges 9b; **Musée Condé:** 12r;
CrusadesWikia: 16r; **Discover Syria:** 26; **Lambeth Palace Library:**
BAL 23c; **Musée de Louvre:** 4r, 17tr; **Walter de Milemete:** 21br;
Munchen StB: Simon Bening/Book of Hours 5b; **Public Domain:**
11tr, 11b, Rashid al Din 27t, Lady of Hats 28, Ismail al Jazari 17l,
Unbekannt 27r; **royalexhibitions.co.uk:** 15c; **Shutterstock:** 10, 27bl,
29l, AMC Photography 15t, Creative Travel Projects 12bl,
Valery Egorov 19b, David Hughes 19t, Natures Moments UK 18,
Billy Stock 25; **Thinkstock:** istockphoto 13t, 13bl, Photos.com 5t, 14bl,
22, 24bl; **Topfoto:** British Library Board 16bl, Fine Art Images/HIP
8bl, 24r, World History Archive 8r; **University of Heidelberg:** 21l.
All other photos, artwork and maps, **Brown Bear Books**.

Brown Bear Books has made every attempt to contact the
copyright holder. If you have any information please contact
licensing@brownbearbooks.co.uk

Library and Archives Canada Cataloguing in Publication

Bow, James, 1972-, author
     Your guide to castles and Medieval warfare / James Bow.

(Destination: Middle Ages)
Includes index.
Issued in print and electronic formats.
ISBN 978-0-7787-2994-5 (hardcover).--
ISBN 978-0-7787-3000-2 (softcover).--
ISBN 978-1-4271-1867-7 (HTML)

     1. Military art and science--History--Medieval, 500-1500--
Juvenile literature. 2. Military history, Medieval--Juvenile literature.
3. Castles--Juvenile literature. I. Title.

D128.B68 2017   j355.009'02   C2016-907397-1
                                             C2016-907398-X

Library of Congress Cataloging-in-Publication Data

Names: Bow, James, author.
Title: Your guide to castles and medieval warfare / James Bow.
Description: New York : Crabtree Publishing Company, [2017] |
     Series: Destination: Middle Ages | Includes index.
Identifiers: LCCN 2016055845 (print) | LCCN 2016056166 (ebook) |
     ISBN 9780778729945 (library binding : alk. paper) |
     ISBN 9780778730002 (pbk. : alk. paper) |
     ISBN 9781427118677 (Electronic HTML)
Subjects: LCSH: Military art and science--History--Medieval,
     500-1500--Juvenile literature. | Castles--Juvenile literature. |
     Sieges--Juvenile literature. | Siege warfare--Juvenile literature. |
     Military history, Medieval--Juvenile literature.
Classification: LCC U37 .B69 2017 (print) | LCC U37 (ebook) |
     DDC 355.409/02--dc23
LC record available at https://lccn.loc.gov/2016055845

Crabtree Publishing Company
www.crabtreebooks.com   1-800-387-7650

Printed in Canada/032017/BF20170111

Published in Canada
Crabtree Publishing
616 Welland Ave.
St. Catharines, ON
L2M 5V6

Published in the United States
Crabtree Publishing
PMB 59051
350 Fifth Avenue, 59th Floor
New York, New York 10118

Published in the United Kingdom
Crabtree Publishing
Maritime House
Basin Road North, Hove
BN41 1WR

Published in Australia
Crabtree Publishing
3 Charles Street
Coburg North
VIC, 3058

Contents

Before We Start

The Roman Empire in Europe was defeated by invaders in 476. The empire split into many kingdoms. Wars became common as these states fought for dominance.

THE AGE OF KNIGHTS

✦ **If you can fight...**

✦ **...get a horse!**

People who could ride a horse and use a weapon were valuable in the new Europe (right). They could easily defeat soldiers on foot. These **knights** helped defend kingdoms. In return, kings gave them land, making them **lords**.

BARBARIANS!

+ **A time of warfare**

+ **Sticking together**

Europe's new kingdoms often fought each other over land and resources. Raiders such as the Vandals, Goths, and Vikings attacked villages. They killed people, and stole crops and livestock. Without the Roman armies to protect them, people struggled to defend themselves.

INTO BATTLE

☛ **Medieval warfare not for wimps**

Wars in the Middle Ages were fought up-close. Soldiers had bows and crossbows, but they mainly fought hand-to-hand (left) with swords and **pikes**. Inventions such as the **stirrup** gave an advantage to knights on horseback. The stirrup held knights steady on their horses, so they could swing their swords at foot soldiers. New metal armor protected them. In **sieges**, soldiers used weapons called catapults that threw large missiles at the walls of castles or fortified towns.

BREAKING NEWS

For protection in dangerous times, Europeans are using the **feudal system**. This system sees society as a pyramid. At the top is the king. Beneath him are the lords, or knights. At the very bottom are the **peasants**. The peasants work for a lord in return for food and protection. The lords promise to fight for the king, in return for land and authority.

PUT YOUR WEAPONS DOWN!

+ Back to the farm

Normal life continued even in times of war. Most soldiers were farmers, so armies often stopped fighting in the fall so men could go home to help with the harvest. Otherwise, there would be no food for the coming year. Campaigns began again in the spring.

Where in the World?

Some of the most important battles of the Middle Ages were fought at the edges of Europe, where Christian Europe clashed with the Islamic and Mongol empires. Other key battles took place within Europe, as rulers fought to increase their territory and power.

ENGLAND

GERMANY

FRANCE

SPAIN

Battle of Hastings, 1066

At the Battle of Hastings, Normans from France, led by William the Conqueror, defeated the forces of King Harold I, who was killed in the battle. William took control of England.

Battle of Tours, 732

Islamic warriors from Spain were advancing into France when their way was blocked by the mounted knights of Charles Martel. Although outnumbered, Martel's troops held off repeated attacks. The Muslims withdrew, and never threatened Western Europe again.

First Crusade, 1095

In 1095, European knights answered the Pope's call to win back control of the Holy City of Jerusalem in the Holy Land. The campaign marked the beginning of over 200 years of fighting between Christians and Muslims for control of the Holy Land.

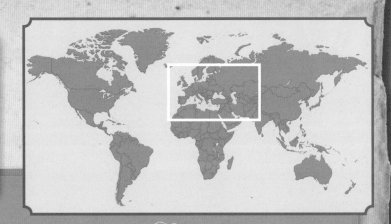

Siege of Orleans, 1429

During the Hundred Years' War between England and France, the French won a decisive victory over the English when they broke the siege of Orléans. The French soldiers were inspired by a peasant girl named Joan of Arc.

RUSSIA

Siege of Constantinople, 1453

The siege and defeat of the capital of the Byzantine Empire by the Ottoman Turks in 1453 is often seen as marking the end of the Middle Ages. The Byzantine Empire of what are now Greece and the Balkans followed the Orthodox Church—a different form of Christianity than the rest of Europe, which followed the Catholic Church.

Constantinople

Battle of Ain Jalut, 1260

The Battle of Ain Jalut was a victory for Muslim forces over Mongols invading from the east. The defeat ended Mongol attacks in the Middle East.

HOLY
LAND

Jerusalem

EGYPT

New Name

After capturing Constantinople, the Ottomans gave the city the name by which it is still known today—Istanbul.

Who We'll Meet

Some of the most influential individuals of the Middle Ages were great warriors. Their military success changed the shape of the world.

SAVIOR OF CHRISTENDOM

+ **Martel stops the invasion**

+ **Wins victory at Tours**

Charles Martel (686–741, right) united the Frankish peoples to create France in 718. In 732, he clashed with the Umayyads. These **Muslims** from Spain were trying to gain land. In the Battle of Tours, Martel's outnumbered forces fought until the Umayyads retreated. The victory halted the advance of Islam into Europe.

First Knights

Charles Martel's forces at Tours included Europe's first mounted knights. The knights helped the small Frankish army resist a series of Umayyad charges.

NEWS FROM AFAR

Born in Mongolia around 1162, Genghis Khan was named Temujin at birth. A fierce warrior, Temujin united the Mongol tribes in 1206 and created an empire. He took the name Genghis Khan, which means "ruler of all," and conquered Siberia, central Asia, and the Middle East. Mongol warriors were masters of a sword called a scimitar (left), and of the bow and arrow on horseback.

FIGHTING THE VIKINGS

- ☛ Alfred saves Wessex...
- ☛ ...but divides England

A prince of the English kingdom of Wessex, Alfred the Great (849–899) fought the Vikings who, by 878, ruled much of England. Alfred surrounded the Vikings and forced them to surrender. He then convinced the Viking king to become a Christian. The two rulers then divided England up between them.

THE SWORD OF ALLAH

- ✦ Khalid fights Islam...
- ✦ ...then helps spread the faith

Khalid Ibn al-Walid (585–642) lived in Arabia during the early days of Islam. Khalid fought against the new religion until he met the Prophet Muhammad. Khalid converted to Islam and became known as "the Sword of Allah." He helped to spread Islam through Arabia and personally led attacks against Byzantine and Persian armies.

THE BLACK PRINCE

- + A military hero

Edward of Woodstock (1330–1376, below) was the son of King Edward III of England. He led English armies in the Hundred Years' War. His victories over France made him a hero. He was named "the Black Prince" in the 1500s, possibly because his shield was black with white feathers.

WARRIOR PRINCESS!

- + Khutulun a wow at war

Khutulun, born in about 1260, was the daughter of a Mongol leader named Kaidu, and the niece of the Mongol emperor Kublai Khan. Khutulun was a warrior, and she rode into battle with her father's armies. She was so famous that the explorer Marco Polo wrote about her in his book about Asia.

A Little Bit of History

The political and economic power of medieval rulers was based on controlling land, so they fought constantly to increase or defend their territory. Constant warfare led to rapid advances in weaponry.

HOLY WARS

✦ **Islam spreads**

✦ **Europeans begin Crusades**

In the early 600s, the prophet Muhammad started preaching a religion called Islam in Arabia. By 640, his followers, called Muslims, had conquered the Middle East and were spreading into Persia and North Africa. By 750, Muslims ruled parts of Spain and Portugal. In 1095, European soldiers began a series of wars called **Crusades**. They wanted to free the Holy City of Jerusalem from Muslim rule. Muslim and Christian forces fought each other for centuries, trying to gain control of land and power. The wars changed Europe and the Middle East forever.

Urban's Call
The Crusades began when Pope Urban II called on European knights to fight for Christians against the Muslim rulers of the Holy Land.

THE HUNDRED YEARS' WAR

+ The war begins

From 1337 to 1453, England and France fought for control of France. Since 1066, when Normans from France had conquered England, the rulers of the two countries had been related. When King Charles IV of France died in 1328, Edward III of England was his closest male relative. The English believed Edward should take the French throne. The French **barons** disagreed—and the Hundred Years' War began.

THE FRENCH RECOVER

+ **England vs France**

+ **The end of the war**

The Hundred Years' War was fought off-and-on for nearly 120 years. Most fighting took place in France. In 1415, a major victory for the English at Agincourt put almost all of France under English rule. But a young woman named Joan of Arc (right) helped **rally** the French to victory. The French pushed English forces out of France for good in 1453.

BREAKING NEWS

The long war between England and France has changed warfare! For the first time, both sides have used full-time soldiers rather than peasants. These troops are trained in weapons such as the English **longbow** (left). To pay for these permanent armies, everyone's taxes will have to go up—sorry!

BANG, BANG, BOOM!

☞ **Gunpowder changes warfare**

☞ **Handguns and artillery**

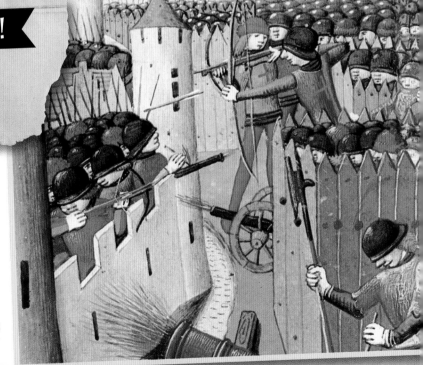

Around 1300, gunpowder reached Europe from China, where it had been invented centuries earlier. Europeans began to use it to fire missiles at the enemy. They invented handguns with long barrels to fire bullets or shot (right), and cannons to fire heavy iron balls. A knight's armor could not stand up to bullets, nor castle walls to cannon fire. Military commanders had to come up with new **tactics** and weapons for defeating the enemy.

A Warlike Society

In a feudal society, everyone had a role to play. For most men, this role included going to war in the service of the nobles who in turn protected the men and their families.

KNOW YOUR PLACE

+ Kings and Barons at the top...

+ ...everyone else at the bottom

Feudal society was a strict hierarchy. People had obligations to serve those above them in society, and to take care of those below them. At the top was the king, followed by nobles who supported him in return for land. Below them were the knights, who provided military service to the nobles in exchange for food, shelter, and protection. Peasants farmed the land of the knights in return for food of their own, shelter, and protection.

WHY GO TO WAR?

☛ Grab as much land as you can...

☛ ...they're not making any more!

One of the major causes of war was to gain territory or to protect it from enemies. In an agricultural society, more land meant more space to grow crops. This allowed the population to grow, making a nation more powerful than smaller neighbors. Land was also essential to the working of the feudal system. Kings used it to reward their nobles, from whom it was distributed to knights, farmers, and peasants.

ABOVE THE KING!

- ✦ **Charlemagne builds an empire**
- ✦ **Brings Europe together**

In the same way that nobles and knights swore loyalty to their king, kings sometimes had to swear loyalty to a more powerful ruler. Charlemagne (right) became king of the Franks in 768, and Holy Roman Emperor in 800. His empire covered much of modern France and Germany. Kings within his territory had to pay him respect and send him taxes called **tribute**.

FIGHTING FOR GOD

- ☞ **Religion a major cause of war**

Most people believed that a king was given the authority to rule by God. Christians and Muslims both believed that God supported their rulers. There was a close link between kings and religious leaders such as the pope (left). Rulers and religious leaders supported the authority of each other.

My Medieval Journal

Imagine you were born into a feudal society in which it was difficult to leave the class into which you were born. Which social groups would you prefer to be born into, and which would be the worst? Give reasons for your preferences.

PASS IT ON!

- ✦ **Live like your parents...**
- ✦ **...for better or worse**

The feudal system was **hereditary**. People inherited their position in society from their parents. The son of a king became king when his father died, and lords passed on lands to their sons. It was hard for people to rise in society, although some peasants used their military skills to become knights. Meanwhile, arguments about who should inherit the throne often started wars.

Knights and Soldiers

Medieval armies were made up of knights, or nobles who fought on horseback, and a larger number of ordinary foot soldiers. Knights and soldiers all fought at close range with the enemy.

MOUNTED KNIGHTS

✦ **A key invention from China**

✦ **Stirrups make fighting possible**

The first knights were Franks led by Charles Martel in the mid-700s. The Franks began to use an invention from China—the stirrup. Stirrups held the rider's feet in place, making him stable enough to be able to swing a sword while on horseback. Knights developed a code of behavior called **chivalry**. This included ideals such as fairness toward other knights and not hurting women or children.

IN THE RANKS

+ **Foot soldiers win wars...**

+ **...but only in large numbers!**

While knights were important fighters, foot soldiers won more battles. Foot soldiers were usually peasants. They had no heavy armor and carried only spears, axes, and shields. They were far cheaper to equip than knights, so armies had hundreds of foot soldiers. In large numbers, they could even overwhelm mounted knights.

BREAKING NEWS

Knights! For the 1200s, why not try a new battlefield style? Throw away those tunics stuffed with horsehair, and even your **chain mail**, and try on a new suit of armor! Now you'll be shielded from swords and arrows with super-strong plates of iron or steel. But make sure your blacksmith makes a suit with plates that are light enough to allow you to move around easily while fighting.

Did you know?

Foot soldiers did not wear chain mail or metal armor. Their only protection was thick leather jackets that were sometimes stuffed with horsehair.

WOMEN AT WAR

☛ **Not all knights were men!**

In the Hundred Years' War, 68 women became members of the Order of the Garter (right), an elite group of knights. In France, female knights helped other knights to prepare for battle or fought themselves. Countries such as Italy and Spain also created special **orders** for female knights. The most famous female knight was Joan of Arc in France.

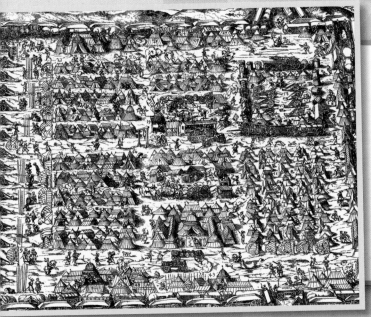

IN THE CAMP

+ Let's all go to the war

Medieval armies attracted crowds of civilian followers. These camp followers included the wives and families of soldiers, as well as people who provided the armies with services. These services included the provision of food, laundry, and weapons. Army camps (left) were like mobile cities that moved from battle to battle.

Holy Warriors

After the fall of the Roman Empire, one of the few sources of power in Europe was the Christian church. Christians soon clashed with a new religion called Islam. Islam began in Arabia and conquered the Holy Land.

THE CRUSADES

+ **Europeans invade the Holy Land**

+ **Set up Crusader states**

In 1095, after Pope Urban II announced the First Crusade, European soldiers set out for the Holy Land. After they captured cities there, they set up "Crusader states," including the Kingdom of Jerusalem. These states were surrounded by enemy territory and so were always ready to fight. None of the states survived for more than 200 years.

THE RELIGIOUS KNIGHTS

✦ **Religious orders protect pilgrims**

Among the European Crusaders in the Holy Land were several special orders of knights. The Knights Templar (left) and the Order of the Holy Sepulchre were set up to protect Christian **pilgrims** visiting the Holy Land. The Knights Hospitaller were a religious military order set up to help pilgrims and Crusaders who were wounded or sick.

NEWS FROM AFAR

In 1202, Pope Innocent III called for Christian armies to recapture Jerusalem from the Muslims. These armies followed the Catholic faith of Christianity. On the way to the Holy Land, they went to Constantinople, the capital of the Byzantine Empire. The Byzantines were also Christians, but they followed the Orthodox Church. The Crusaders **sacked** the city (right) and set up their own empire.

POWERFUL ENEMIES

- Muslim leaders eye Holy Land
- Clash with Crusaders

The Crusaders faced an enemy inspired by the Islamic faith and led by outstanding generals. Saladin (left) had conquered Syria in 1185, and fought hard to take the cities of the Holy Land. Later, the general Qutuz led Egypt's Mamluk armies in victories against both the Crusaders (1250) and the Mongols (1260).

QUEEN OF THE HOLY CITY

+ Sibylla goes to war...

+ ...but cannot defeat Saladin

Sibylla became queen of the Holy Kingdom of Jerusalem in 1186, after the death of the previous king, her son Baldwin V. When her husband, Guy, was captured by Saladin in 1187, Sibylla personally led the defense of Jerusalem against the Muslim armies. After the city fell, Saladin allowed her to escape to Tripoli. In 1189, Sibylla joined Guy in his siege of Acre, the only Crusader State that had not fallen to Saladin. Sibylla died of disease in the camp outside the city in 1190.

Castle Building

Castles were the strongholds of monarchs and nobles. These fortified centers were widely built between 1000 and 1300 as protection from enemy attack.

Government

Monarchs governed from their castles. Other castles belonged to barons who acted as the king's local officers. Barons collected taxes and enforced the law.

MOTTE AND BAILEY

+ The earliest castles

+ Built on hills

The earliest castles used a design called motte and bailey. A wooden or stone fortification, or keep, was built on top of a hill called a motte. The motte gave defenders an advantage over the attackers fighting their way up the hill. The hill stood inside an enclosed courtyard called a bailey. The bailey was surrounded by a wall of pointed wooden stakes called a palisade, which could stab any attacker trying to climb over.

BREAKING NEWS

Update your castle now! Our tip is to use stone rather than wood for your buildings—stone does not burn. Be sure to include a strong fortified tower, called a keep. This is a tall, rectangular tower that can be defended even if the castle falls. Ensure you have room to govern your lands. You'll need to collect taxes and judge disputes, so include a room where you can meet with the public. And don't forget a big **dungeon**. Castles are often used to hold prisoners.

BUILT FOR DEFENSE

✦ **Strong walls...**

✦ **...and high battlements**

As stone castles replaced wooden motte-and-bailey castles, thick stone walls replaced wooden palisades. Battlements at the top of the wall allowed defenders to fire down at any attackers from behind stone risers, or merlons. Thin slit-windows in the walls allowed archers to shoot out without getting shot. Walls were often built in **concentric** rings. Any attackers who scaled the first wall were then trapped between the walls, making them easy targets.

DON'T GET WET!

☛ **The water feature every castle needs?**

☛ **Looks lovely, but can be deadly!**

Some castles were surrounded by a moat, or a deep ditch filled with water. Knights in heavy armor could drown if they tried to cross it. The water went right up to the walls. This kept any attackers at a distance. The moat was crossed by a **drawbridge**. The bridge could be pulled up, so the castle was easy to defend.

ENTER HERE

✦ **Gateways are weak points...**

✦ **...so they are heavily guarded**

The weakest point of any castle was the gate that allowed people in. The gate was often protected by a drawbridge that was raised to keep attackers out. A strong, heavy barrier called a portcullis also slid down between grooves in the walls to block the gate. "Murder holes" above the gate allowed defenders to drop heavy stones or boiling oil on any attackers trying to break through the entrance gate below them.

Sieges and Siege Engines

Sieges were key to medieval warfare. Attackers surrounded a castle or town, and tried to make it surrender through force—or by waiting for the defenders to starve.

SIEGE ENGINES

☛ Scaling the walls...

☛ ...or knocking them down

Attackers used a number of ways to attack a walled town or castle. Engineers built large machines known as siege engines. Attackers cut down trees and made battering rams to bash their way through gates or walls. They used tall ladders to scale walls, or built wheeled towers that they could push up against the walls. Soldiers inside the tower could jump on to the battlements on top of the walls. Attackers also used catapults or trebuchets (right). These machines used weights and levers to fling huge stones or flaming wood at, or sometimes over, the walls of a castle or town.

DISEASE AND DESTRUCTION

✦ Inhabitants lack food

✦ Become sick easily

People locked up inside a besieged town or castle usually had little food. They grew weak and easily became sick. Fatal diseases such as cholera and typhus spread easily. In 1346, Mongols besieged the city of Kaffa in the Crimea. When their own soldiers died from **plague**, the Mongols threw the bodies over the walls into Kaffa. The disease then spread among the city's inhabitants.

> *"During this business the king had carpenters construct a fearful engine called the Warwolf, and this when it threw, brought down the whole wall."*

Contemporary account of the Siege of Stirling Castle in Scotland by King Edward I in 1304.

MY MEDIEVAL JOURNAL

Imagine you are trapped inside a medieval siege. You think you can find a way to escape, but it might be dangerous. What sort of arguments would you use to try to persuade your family or friends to risk their lives and escape with you?

INSIDE A SIEGE

+ **You can fight back...**

+ **...but it's no fun!**

During a siege, defenders guarded the fortress walls. They pushed over attackers' ladders, and dropped stones or boiling oil on the enemy below (left). People trapped inside soon ran short of food, and some died from starvation or disease. Bodies piled up inside the fortress, creating a terrible smell. Often during a siege, nothing happened. Sometimes people got bored and lost the will to resist.

BREAKING NEWS

A big change in the 1200s! A new weapon has appeared in Europe (right). This cannon uses gunpowder to fire huge stones and iron balls at great speeds. No castle walls can withstand their force. Could this be the end for castles?

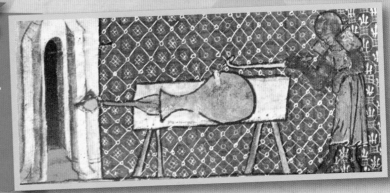

Life on Campaign

On campaign, armies sometimes traveled long distances to fight. When they reached their destination, life was often brutal for civilians as well as soldiers.

GETTING TO THE FIGHTING

+ **Walking to war...**

+ **...is the slow way**

While knights rode their horses on campaign, foot soldiers had to walk. Supplies such as food and weapons were carried in trains of wagons pulled by oxen. Most roads were dirt tracks, so it was slow going. Armies often built barges to float men and supplies down rivers. When wars were fought far away, such as the Crusades in the Holy Land, boats carried armies across the sea (above).

CAUGHT IN THE CROSSFIRE

☛ **Local civilians suffer**

☛ **Populations butchered**

Civilians often suffered during medieval warfare. Armies stole supplies from farmers and villagers, no matter whose side they were on. This caused shortages and suffering. Some commanders even ordered soldiers to kill everyone in a city, including women and children. This was meant to send a message to other cities to not resist an attack.

WAR DOCTORS

☛ Surgeons on the battlefield

The best medical care for soldiers was provided by the Byzantine and Islamic empires. Their armies were accompanied by skilled surgeons who were used to dealing with battlefield wounds. The European Crusaders, on the other hand, relied on warrior-monks known as the Knights of St. John, or the Hospitallers. They took care of the wounded, but they were not trained physicians.

DON'T GET HURT!

+ Medical care is poor

In battle, opposing knights and soldiers fought in close combat. They broke skulls, cut each other with swords, and stabbed each other with spears. It was almost impossible for wounded men to escape from the fighting. Many knights fought on after being wounded, even with arrows sticking out of them.

GRAB WHAT YOU CAN!

✦ Looters grab valuables...
✦ ...as a form of pay

After a battle or siege, the victors often looted the enemy camp or city (left). Soldiers stole what they wanted and attacked anyone who got in their way. Looting was seen as a form of reward for the soldiers. In the late 1400s, German soldiers called *Landsknecht* created a new fashion by wearing all the tattered clothes they had stolen at the same time.

Fighting for Power

Many wars that took place in the Middle Ages had lasting consequences. Nations rose and fell in importance depending on their military success, and different rulers came to power.

Execution

Prisoners of war were usually freed in return for a payment, or ransom. After the siege of Acre, however, both sides killed their prisoners.

THE THIRD CRUSADE

☞ Europe's kings go to war

The Third Crusade (1189–1192) was an attempt by Europeans to recapture Jerusalem from the Muslim forces of Saladin. The English and French kings and the Holy Roman Emperor all joined the campaign, which is sometimes called the King's Crusade. Although the Crusaders captured cities such as Acre (right), they failed to capture Jerusalem. Saladin agreed to allow Christian pilgrims to enter the city. Christians briefly ruled Jerusalem in the 1200s, but otherwise it remained in Muslim hands throughout the Crusades.

BREAKING NEWS

England's King John has been fighting a civil war against his barons. In return for agreeing to let him raise money from the people to fight the French, the barons have forced him to sign the Magna Carta ("Great Charter") in 1215. The charter gives the English people basic legal rights. The Magna Carta can't stop the civil war, but the signing of the document might mark the start of English **democracy**.

THE CONQUEST OF WALES

☞ Edward of England takes control

Wales and England had been separate kingdoms. In 1277, the English king Edward I invaded Wales. After five years of fighting, Edward defeated the Welsh army at the Battle of Orewin Bridge. He built castles along the border to help control the Welsh, and settled English peasants in Wales. The English **parliament** let him raise taxes to pay for the conquest. But in return, Edward had to give parliament more say in running the kingdom.

My Medieval Journal

Imagine you are a rebel trying to break into a medieval castle. Using the information and pictures of castles in this book, see if you can figure out any weaknesses in castle defenses. Are there any obvious ways to get inside?

Did you know?

Chepstow Castle (right) was built on cliffs above the Wye River on the Welsh border. The bathrooms hung out over the cliffs, so that waste fell into the river below.

THE WARS OF THE ROSES

+ Families in conflict

The Wars of the Roses in England lasted for 30 years, from 1455 to 1485. The House, or family, of Lancaster fought the House of York for the English throne. The Lancaster family symbol was a red rose. Eventually, the Lancasters were victorious. Henry VII became king and married Elizabeth of York to unite the families. Their son, Henry VIII, founded the Tudor **dynasty**. He and his daughter, Queen Elizabeth I, ruled over a long period of prosperity in England.

The Great Warriors

Many of the warriors who changed the course of the Middle Ages are still famous. Some were great commanders, while others were just in the right place at the right time.

Meeting

Although this painting shows Saladin and Richard I together, most historians believe that they never actually met face to face.

FROM SOLDIER TO SULTAN

+ **Saladin fights the Crusaders**

+ **Founds Ayyubid dynasty**

Born in Armenia, Saladin joined the Syrian army and rose to rule Egypt in the 1100s. He fought the Crusaders in the Holy Land and later founded the Ayyubid dynasty, which ruled Egypt, Syria, and North Africa. He fought King Richard I of England during the Third Crusade. The two rivals agreed (above) that Jerusalem should stay in Muslim hands, but be open to Christian pilgrims from all over the world.

FIGHTING FRENCHMAN

◆ **Raynald fights Saladin**

Raynald of Châtillon led the Kingdom of Antioch which was set up during the First Crusade. He built a small fleet of ships to raid Muslim settlements on the Red Sea, and he fought against Saladin at the Siege of Kerak in 1183. But when he attacked Saladin again four years later, the Christian army was crushed. Saladin himself cut off Raynald's head.

SON OF THE GREAT KHAN

✦ Ögedei follows Dad's example

The Mongol Empire founded by Genghis Khan grew rapidly after his death. In the early 1200s, his son Ögedei Khan (left) conquered Persia, Armenia, and China. He attacked Korea and India. Mongol forces marched into Europe, conquering the Rus of modern-day Russia, and defeating Poland and Hungary. Ögedei ordered his soldiers farther into Europe. When he died in 1241, however, they retreated and went home to build him a monument. Ögedei's family quarreled over who would take over the throne, and the Mongols never returned to Europe.

THE LIONHEART

☞ An English hero...
☞ ...who rarely visited England

King of England from 1189 to 1199, Richard I (right) was known as "the Lionheart" for his courage. He led an army at the age of 16. He was one of the Christian leaders of the Third Crusade. He forced Saladin to allow pilgrims into Jerusalem. During his reign, Richard spent less than six months in England. He was always away fighting crusades in the Holy Land.

THE MAID OF FRANCE

+ Visions of victory

Joan of Arc started seeing visions as a child. She believed God wanted her to drive the English from France. During the Hundred Years' War, she led French forces to victory at the Siege of Orléans in 1429. Joan was captured and killed by the English in 1431. However, the victory changed the course of the war. France had the advantage, and won the final victory in 1453.

Decisive Battles

Clashes such as those between France and England in the Hundred Years' War, or between Europeans and Muslims in the Crusades, helped shape a new world that was growing larger and more international.

STOPPING THE UMAYYADS

+ **Charles Martel stands firm**

At Tours in north-central France in 732, Charles Martel's 15,000 Frankish soldiers fought up to 50,000 soldiers from the Islamic Umayyad **caliphate** in Spain. Martel's men were outnumbered, but were heavily armored and well trained. They resisted repeated Umayyad cavalry charges. Worried about the coming winter, the Umayyads retreated. The victory halted the advance of Islamic armies into Europe. They never threatened western Europe again.

BATTLE FOR ENGLAND

✦ **The Normans invade...**

✦ **...and found a new dynasty**

In 1066, the Anglo-Saxon King Harold I marched north to defeat Viking invaders at the Battle of Stamford Bridge. Then he heard that Norman invaders from France were heading for England. The Norman prince, William, claimed that he was the rightful ruler of England. Harold marched south and met the Normans in the Battle of Hastings (right). The English fought off Norman attacks until Harold was killed. His leaderless army collapsed. William claimed the throne and began a new period of Anglo-Norman history. He is still known as William the Conqueror.

" I have persecuted its native inhabitants beyond all reason... I have cruelly oppressed them... "

William the Conqueror describes his conquest of the English in 1066

NEWS FROM AFAR

Islamic forces and Crusaders worked together to defeat Mongol invaders in the Holy Land. The Muslims and the Mongols fought in the Battle of Ain Jalut in 1260. Crusaders from Acre provided supplies to the Muslim Mamluk warriors led by Qutuz. Qutuz's forces destroyed the Mongols. The defeat stopped the Mongol advance in the Middle East once and for all.

NEW TECHNOLOGY WINS THE DAY

☞ Longbow vs crossbow

At the Battle of Crécy in 1346 during the Hundred Years' War, 12,000 English soldiers defeated 30,000 French troops. The victory was partly due to the longbow. The weapon fired arrows farther than the French **crossbow**. It took more skill to use, but the trained English archers could fire faster than the French. The battle helped the English to conquer Calais, which they held until 1558.

Did you know?

In the Siege of Constantinople in 1453, an Ottoman army used a huge cannon called Basilica to destroy the city walls. The Byzantine Empire fell.

A NEW AGE

+ Europeans look toward the sea

The Fall of Constantinople in 1453 ended the Middle Ages. The Muslim Ottomans controlled the routes to the Holy Land, so further crusades were impossible. Cannons and guns had made armor and castles **obsolete**. The Turks controlled land trade routes to Asia. Europeans looked to the sea to find another way to get to Asia—which led to the discovery of America.

Glossary

barons The most important nobles in a country

caliphate An area ruled by a Muslim caliph

chain mail A coat made of tiny metal rings joined together

chivalry A code of behavior and values that guided the actions of medieval knights

concentric Describes a circle or other shape inside a larger circle or shape

crossbow A weapon with a handle and a cross strut that fires arrows or bolts

Crusades A series of military campaigns by European Christians against Muslims in the Holy Land

democracy A system of government in which the people elect people to represent them

drawbridge A bridge that can be pulled up

dungeon An underground prison cell

dynasty A series of rulers who all come from the same family

feudal system A way to organize society in which everyone has set roles

hereditary Describes something passed from parents to their children

knights Men who served their lords or monarch as mounted soldiers in wartime

longbow A large, powerful bow used to shoot arrows

lords In the feudal system, nobles granted land by the king

Muslims Followers of the Islamic religion

obsolete Out of date and useless

orders Societies of knights who follow particular rules

parliament In the Middle Ages, a body of lords who advised rulers on making new laws

peasants Poor farmers who were the lowest level of medieval society

pikes Long wooden poles with points on the end, used as weapons

pilgrims People who make a journey for a religious purpose

plague A highly contagious and serious disease

rally To urge troops to carry on fighting

sack To rob and destroy a town

sieges Military actions in which attackers surround a castle or city

stirrup A loop for the foot of a horse rider

tactics Plans for fighting a battle

tribute A payment made by one ruler to another on whose support he or she depends

September 4: The Roman Empire in the West ends with the fall of Rome.

October 10: At the Battle of Tours, Frankish knights defeat an Islamic invasion of Europe.

The First Crusade begins when European knights travel to fight Muslims in the Holy Land.

Genghis Khan unites the Mongols and begins building an empire through military strength.

476   640   732   1066   1095   1189   1206

Muslim warriors have conquered much of the Middle East and converted it to Islam.

October 14: William the Conqueror wins the Battle of Hastings and becomes ruler of England.

The Third Crusade fails to recapture Jerusalem from the Muslims.

On the Web

www.ducksters.com/history/middle_ages/knight_armor_and_weapons.php
Visit this site for more information about medieval knights, and their armor and weapons.

medieval-castles.org/index.php/medieval_warfare_reading
A menu page with links to many articles about medieval castles and warfare.

www.historyforkids.net/the-crusade.html
A guide to the Crusades and their effect on Europe and the Middle East.

www.bbc.co.uk/history/british/middle_ages/hundred_years_war_01.shtml
An introduction to the Hundred Years' War from the BBC History site.

www.medievalchronicles.com/medieval-battles-wars/medieval-battles-timeline/
A detailed timeline of the major military campaigns, battles, and sieges of the Middle Ages.

Books

Bruce, Julia. *Siege!: Can You Capture a Castle?* (Step into History). Enslow Publishers, 2009.

Jeffrey, Gary. *Crusades* (Graphic Medieval History). Crabtree Publishing Company, 2014.

Jones, Molly. *Medieval Knights* (Ancient Warriors). Child's World, 2015.

Lassieur, Allison. *Medieval Knight Science: Armor, Weapons, and Siege Warfare* (Warrior Science). Capstone Press, 2016.

Macdonald, Fiona. *You Wouldn't Want to Be Joan of Arc!: A Mission You Might Want to Miss.* Franklin Watts, 2010.

Murrell, Deborah. *Weapons* (Medieval Warfare). Gareth Stevens Publishing, 2008.

September 3: Crusaders support Muslim forces to defeat Mongol invaders at the Battle of Ain Jalut.

April 30: The Hundred Years' War begins between England and France.

April 29: Joan of Arc inspires the French to victory at Orléans, a decisive battle in the Hundred Years' War.

May 29: Islamic Ottoman Turks conquer Constantinople, ending the Byzantine Empire.

1260 · **1277** · **1337** · **1415** · **1429** · **1453** · **1455**

Edward I invades Wales, which he conquers and makes part of his kingdom.

October 25: English archers help win a great victory in the Battle of Agincourt.

July 17: The Hundred Years' War ends in victory for France.

May 22: The Wars of the Roses begin in England.

Index

A
Agincourt 11
Ain Jalut, Battle of 7, 29
Alfred the Great 9
Antioch 26
armor 15
Ayyubid dynasty 26

B
battles 6–7, 28–29
Black Prince 9
Byzantine Empire 7, 16, 17, 23, 29

C
camp followers 15
campaign, military 22–23
castles 11, 18–19, 21, 25
Charlemagne 13
Charles IV of France 10
chivalry 14
civilians in wartime 22, 23
Constantinople 7, 17, 29
Crécy, Battle of 29
Crusader states 16, 17
Crusades 6, 10, 16–17, 22, 23, 24, 25, 29

E
Edward III, King 9
Egypt 26
England 6, 7, 9, 10, 24, 25, 28

F
feudal system 5, 12, 13, 23
First Crusade 26
foot soldiers 14–15, 22, 23
Fourth Crusade 17
France 7, 10, 27

G H
Goths 4
government 18
gunpowder 11, 21
Harold I, King 28
Hastings, Battle of 6, 28
Henry VIII 25
Holy Land 6, 10, 16, 17, 22, 26, 27, 29
Holy Roman Emperor 13
horses 5, 8, 22
Hundred Years' War 7, 10, 11, 15, 27, 29

I J
Islam 6, 8, 9, 10, 17, 24, 29
Jerusalem 10, 16, 17, 24, 27
Joan of Arc 11, 15, 27
John, King 24

K L
Khan, Genghis 8, 27
Khan, Ögedia 27
Khutulun 9
knights 4, 5, 8, 12, 14–15, 16, 22, 23
Knights Hospitaller 16, 23
Knights of St. John 23
Knights Templar 16
land 4, 12
Landsknecht 23
longbow 11, 29
looting 23

M N
Magna Carta 24
Mamluks 29
Martel, Charles 6, 8, 14, 28
Mongols 7, 8, 9, 20, 27, 29
Muhammad 9, 10

My Medieval Journal 13, 21, 25
Normans 6, 10

O
Order of the Garter 15
Orléans, Siege of 7, 27
Ottoman Turks 7, 29

P Q R
peasants 12
pilgrims 24, 27
Qutuz 17, 29
Raynald of Châtillon 26
religion 13
Richard I 26, 27
Roman Empire 4

S
Saladin 17, 24, 26, 27
Sibylla 17
siege engines 20
sieges 5, 20–21
society 12–13
Spain 8, 10, 28
stirrup 5, 14

T
Third Crusade 24, 25, 26, 27
Tours, Battle of 6, 8, 28
transportation 22
Tudor Dynasty 25

U V W
Umayyads 8, 28
Urban II, Pope 10, 16
Vandals 4
Vikings 4
Wales 25
Wars of the Roses 25
weapons 5, 11, 29
William the Conqueror 6, 28